"Let your light so shine before men that they may see your good works, and glorify your father which is in heaven"
    MATTHEW 5:16

THE METAMORPHI OF THE PHENOMENI vol.3

Poetry by

Edward Scott

vol. 1 "No Reasonable Explanation Required"
vol. 2 "The Afterbirth"

ISBN: 1-4033-2456-5 (e-book)
ISBN: 1-4033-2457-3 (Paperback)

This book is printed on acid free paper.

Artwork (cover) by: Jimmie Hayes Scott entitled
The Metamorphli
Additional poetry by: The artist; Joyce Ervin and
James Scott (A victim of Scottism)

1stBooks – rev. 02/26/03

"Ye are the light of the world
A city that is set on a hill
cannot be hid"

MATTHEW 5:14

Foreword

*The Metamorphi of the Phenomeni is
about the levels of incarnate change,
blessed through God's forgiveness,
that we are allowed to travel
through.
To search that level of oneness of the
mind, body, and soul.
Does not the caterpillar crawl to the
metamorphosis of flight,
Does not the day metamorphi into
the soliloquy of night,
So stands the phenomeni called
man, from the womb the metamorphi
begins.
We crawl to walk, run, and race to
new levels of being, where living,
loving, and learning how is the
ultimate thing.
Ending up we reach out for one
divine spiritual reality, to overcome
the negativity of the sphere which
is evil.
Fore which there is the individual
common level of good under one
truly righteous
Son.
In which I surrender on to you,*

the
'METAMORPHI OF THE PHENOMENI'

In Loving Memory
of
Kelvon Timothy Scott
1963-1995
Rest In Peace

Acknowledgments

Thank you God!

Fore
Edwina, Edjuan, Paris, Evron, Ashley, Apithany,
Jimmie, and Kimmie

Fore
Pastor Carol Hughes, Reverend Walter Jackson & his
wife, plus all of his congregation at:
New Jerusalem Baptist Church
1501 Peralta street
West Oakland, California 94607

& Pastor Boyd Patterson

Fore not for your inspirations and motivations,
this book would not exist.

And last but not least, Thank You!
Joyce Ervin & Charles Scott,
the proof that 1+1 does not always equal 2,
but in your case it equaled M.E.
(The Mysterious Element)

THE METAMORPHI OF THE PHENOMENI vol.3

"Trust in the Lord with all your heart and lean not on your own understanding."

PROVERBS 3:5

"In all your ways acknowledge him and he shall direct your path."

PROVERBS 3:6

Table of Contents

I'll Never Love Again

I am so tired of this myth
called love
I've seen the fear's it's
clouded with tears, and
I believe it's somewhere
up above
A big hearted person caring
for this reason or that
stuck with a never ending
void of lost love, and emotional
regret
A wasted time of pure energy
of body, mind, and soul
I'll never love again, it's too
easy to hurt that which is
gold
Should be a never ending
beginning to a nursery rhyme
All real lovers end up doing is
crying, trying time
Why I ask, Why me GOD
just show me where your love
should be with your ethereal nod
And after all this time, I thought
I knew, the ups, and downs, the
ins, and outs, but I just don't
have a clue, to be as good as
you

Eclipse

Only as a concept before time
could I subconsciously be
deceived
By the consciousness of a love
I never knew
Natures creed of a planted seed
with a bottom line desire for
You
Upon a love so far, but yet so near
let rivers run, mountains slope, and
valleys detour not a thought so
clear
Adolescent marvels of life, feelings
that fainted heartbeats whisper
fore the things I would do just to be
with you
find the strongest of men weak with
shameless unspoken censure
Just to want you, just to touch you,
just to hold you in my heart
Just to squeeze, and caress you endlessly
as timeless gestures start
To kiss the luscious passions of your
lovely, rosy, juicy lips
Is the creed of a planted seed, as two
becomes one nocturnal
eclipse

Medulla Flux

As I run from my
maker
an unforeseen
illusion
Stacked upon the
neck of the blemished, of
a subliminal confusion
Collisions called dysfunction's
of illusions vexed
There's no escape
as he be of me
which is of he, and
the simple is so
complexed

The Big-O, Big-O

The Big-O she sometimes acts
sleazy, and loving her isn't
always easy
With her big shapely port like
thighs, she greets all the fleets
just to make wills turn, and her
friends are in the street, let the
simple souls burn
So lets talk about her new breast
implants from a federal trick, tits
of the city, watch out, stand
back!
The whore is working E Pluribus
Unum, you know one of many
When she was young the Big-Os
hip like streets carried people
all night and day, up and about
the great Broadway
She had one lover in which I
thought she showed care, his
name was Jack London, and she
called him square
The Big-O somewhat of a deity I
hail, until one day she had me
strung out, and locked up in
jail, so beyond the vale we tole a
tale of the melting pot
discriminately boiling over, with
the same olde folkes running
from some wasted thing, of
histories unleashed rover
The Big-O a glorious, glitzy
affair, very serious when raising

her dress like taxes to live
She just sometimes desires to
much of the mind, body, and
heart, and with hers it's hard to
give

Edward Scott

Lies Upon Skin

*Sometimes
beauty on the
outside
just lies upon
skin*

*A deception of
the ugly deep
with in*

*But if from the
inside it breaks
and seethes
out*

*Declare a true
substance of
love*

*In need of no
superficial
doubt*

Revenge Is A Drink Called Suicide

Revenge is a drink
best served on the
rocks

Twisted minds that
are in some clocks
A matter of the mirror
it sometimes unlocks

Poured, it shakes, and
stirs to unmasked the
deep rooted master
it inevitably
serves

Sour seeded, bitter tasting
it goes down smooth, fore
hatred is tending the bar
that emotions
entertain

And feelings serving up the
last round with notions of
doom, and only suicide to
gain

Edward Scott

Metamorphi

For the concept
of a lover's
view

Just to stay in
touch

Such a hard living
we do

It's the values
of simple things

In need of so
much

The Fit

You are the path that I must
take to recreate, and if I opposedly
stray I still must pay,

Fore you are the lock, and I am
the key, allow me to loose myself
upon the secrets of a passion
flowers bloom so intimately

If ever there was a dream so true
by any other name, the dreams I
dream would be definitely of you
with only my lust to blame

Let me come inside the mind of
deep raptures of lovely, luscious
moments that captures the heart
and eclipse the soul

Fore you are the lock, and I am
the key, allow me timeless bliss to
be or not to be

Let time be the essence of a love I
adore, forever knowing the choice was
always yours

Your ethereal essence was of love
from the start, until ultimately you
begin to unlock my hear

Edward Scott

The Brown Nose On The Black Face

Is it the creed of
cultivated greed amongst a
people, who against all odds
still try to succeed

And what is with this racism
within a race, and when, and
where did it first take place

I find it hard to comprehend,
when the worst progress in
negativity comes from your
own so called kin

It's such a terrible fact, but the
truth is in the way that your own
people act

So beware of the profound
disgrace, and watch for the brown
nose on the neo-nazi with the
black face

Do You're Due

*When I come for you remember why
how you stomped, whooped, and beat
up father, and then hung him behind
a lie
When I come for you, it will be like
no other, you've sold drugs to your
brother's, and sister's, and betrayed
even your mother
When I come for you, you will
remember your due, and pray for
forgiveness before I'm through
When I come for you it will be to late
you'll reap what you've sown as
I deliver your fate*

Edward Scott

THE UNVEILING

*Tell me a story of a long
time ago,
About who, what, and why
the mysteries of his-stories
that I don't
know
Covert here for a fluxed
learned affliction,
truth of true beings is
stranger than fiction
Knowledge is power that's
The glory of it all,
tell a lie long enough, and
watch to see who
fall*

The Cost Of A Holocaust

Red, red, who swung dead, that man
who cried before the popular tree
not me, must have been his-story
trickling down for the world to see
So their strange fruit I will not be
swinging lifeless in that unpopular
tree
From the atrocities of yesteryear
a curse so far but yet so near
What yonder programmed mind
breaks a windows view, it reaches
the depths of souls still sleep, and
yet not a clue
Beaten blue, labeled colored, coon,
spook, jungle bunny, spear chunking
sambo, Afro-American nigger
To a Negro African American being
set to avoid the true inheritance of
Pharaohs king
So imagine the unimaginable,
imaginably misled, yes let the blood of
my roots boil a course through his-
stories head, and when it comes to evil
inhumane injustice of apathetic
mistreatment of years dead
Heres to the perverted liberty of
freedom, from an ancestral dis-ease
label me
red

Edward Scott

Color Guards

*Power is not in the shedding
of a blood to be buried by a
crypt
Tis the knowledge of kings
that cut like a knife are you
hip
One should choose to bloom
from the knowledge nurtured
naturally, and miss the color
seed planted
To choose the greatest gift of
wasting nobody, and give all the
love God's granted
Killing a nothing for something
some say OK, but killing
something for nothing just ain't
the way
Brutality is the lesson learned,
and dying a reality that's hard
Though if you are love you 'll get
your turn, to teach a change of
the color
guard*

Suffering Righteously

*Suffering, suffering, and nobody
to see, I guess to suffer the blame
is on me*

*Lonely lost liberties, masked by my
righteous soul of true being*

*In a world where I don't belong, the
feelings just won 't subside*

*A common goal for liberty, I will
not be denied*

*So who loses for a righteous song
when lovers' hearts collide*

Elementary Times

Distant drums of adolescents
where hot winds whined, to
the beat of highs, buy's and
cries
As I regress in minds
I digress to elementary times
fore innocents was just there
now the wondering has left
me all alone, with only my
soul to bare
Time waits for no one, so
they say, never did I think
I would feel or be this way
Outcome of income I live to
see, as I struggle with the
blessings of a brand new
me

Absorbed

*I've seen great big men
go down in bottles
transgressing from deep
within
Waking up to absolute
sublived loneliness they
go down in search of a
friend
like a shipwrecked captive
lost in a sea of suffering
trying to meet his
end
Just to find nothing that's
real or free, and wondering
where it all
began*

Edward Scott

I Have A Dream, That Reparations Screamed

It is about yesterday, and
where I've been, It is about time and space
and a soul stirred to wake within
    It is about money, tossing
and turning up with who, what, and why
Dying before true knowledge fills the
cup a life full of crying
    It is about tennis shoe pimps
and you hoe everytime you wear their name
they should shell out the dough
    It's about followers and
leaders monkey see, monkey due wake up
check your program, and we'll see who 's who
    It's about all I've said,
and more Power of knowledge, it's the key to
unlock the treasures held captive beyond
the door
    It's about the middle passage
America's biggest score in which time will not
forget but still there's so much more
    It's about slavery, beatings
and lynchings yet the raping of a people, and
obligations unmet
    It's about time which has not
healed, fore the truth has yet to be revealed
    It's about denial of the beast
from it's own brood, as they revel in the
feast thinking the harvest was shrewd
    It's about good and evils, forced
distorted sight to mask as we enter the race of black
and white

       It's about Kings, Queens, and their robber
barons of immoral begotten booty
       It's about the gene's of your biological
blend
       It's about confusing good and bad by the
color of your skin
       It's about celebrations because
program tells you when to spend through
your children, break the merchants trend
       It's about Medger, Malcolm, and
Martin, who told the naked truth about the
feces of a species who's chickens have come
home to roost
       It's about chemical warfare, and
many a Tuskeegee experiments done with no
regret, this is the power of education, so
please never forget
       I had a dream reparations
screamed at all who must pay their
debt

Ways And Means

*Genes don't care who
ware them
living low while kissing
the sky*

*Seeing people just as
they are
and then we wonder
why*

*Life is to live
like love is to
give*

*This we learn, and
try, recreated in ways that
are mean, we live for
love or die*

*Howling at moons, out
of control, racing about
rooms, just before your
light zooms in*

*Then you pray after
the stray, and still there
is no earthly
friend*

*Genes don't care who
ware them
though some may want
a glance*

Recreated in ways that
are mean
now lets give love
a chance

One Plus One Is Not Always Two

There has only been
one immaculate conception
we both find
true
If I be of he
and you be of me,
does that not make our
conception immaculate
too
And though you put
life in love, as I put
life in you
We are the divine
truth that 1+1
is not always 2
The gift God gave
you as a present
to me
I will love forever
with all my heart and
soul beyond
eternity

The Unveiling, Raising Up Americas Dress

America,
my cup runneth over, and
some are over due

Stop eating, beating, and
cheating your young
turning them old, and blue

Take care of that, which
takes care of you, before it's
to late and you get your due

Dr. Quack is pimping, him
and his H.M.O.s, while Mary's
little lamb is pregnant blowed
up by the vapors of U.F.O.s

Everyday people we've only
just begun to live, love, and
learn

Fore the battle is sometimes
over and done, but the war for
spiritual discovery is where the
victory is
one

Edward Scott

The Lusting For Imperial Repute (Cry Hooker)

I want an old hooker that's crisp,
fresher than cornflakes, and milk
One thats naturally clean, and
looks good under the silk

I want an old hooker who knows
what to do, an imperial old hooker
whose wise, and true
One thats refined mentally, and
physically like 14 karat gold
One thats not too concerned about
being bought or sold

I want an old hooker who knows
knowledge is key, and education is
power
One thats not just stimulated every 5
minutes on the hour
One that can cook while in bed, and
use her head, you know! an old
hooker who's well read
I want an old hooker that's looking
to be all good, not one that's been
had by the whole neighborhood

I want an old hooker rich, and vile,
ruthless when broke
One that stands not just for money,
but for me when it comes to a down
stroke

Justice when it comes to our time,
and a smile for me, me, me, me,
mine
I want an old hooker, no more of
ill repute
An old hooker who's willing and ready
to bare my fruit

Love Rules

The rules were made to be
broken, for a selected few, and
if I'm wrong
Let heaven, and nature balance
the reasons for my
song
For we are all on a journey
from the apocalypse, in search
of one light of divine
spirituality that is
true
The trials, and tribulations are
meant to be, fore lovers life is
due
And under one Son for which
life stands, thy kingdom come
on you
too
So strong is the dust, from which
wisdom came, so weak is the spirit
where life has no
gain
Fore in one reality for which it
stands true, the rules of love
are not just for a chosen
few

Frowns Clowns Mask

Have you ever looked
deep into the face of
madness
A sordid irrational kind
of sadness
Fore if you are a judge
of race, creed, and
style
Beware of the deep rooted
dangers masked by a
smile

E Pluribus Unum

I journeyed to the temple honored
for a chance to meet, and succeed
A woman who has the worlds
respect, inwhich I paid indeed

I met a woman named Angelou
A gifted poet was she, she stood
upon the podium, and poetry flowed
all about me

So as she amazed, and dazzeled the
crowd, a response of hands slapping
fiercely, and loud

Let me know of the talent given was
spiritually true, a blessing by God,
and hers as well too

So when I got my chance to meet
her, my books a gift I too share
She looked right down, and shook
her head as though my books were
not there

A shock to my systems talent, my
motivator wrecked my soul, I envisioned
a person selfishly set, as the ego she
purely stole

So to the fan who admires gifts
righteously sent from above, watch
out for the people who you support
cause it's money they really love

God's Complexed Simplicity

God's equation for love
was multiplied by one
individuals effort in
the flesh

And the sacrifice was
for universal love
an immaculate conception
under the moon, the stars,
the sun

A universal gift, for he's
blessed us beyond
imagination, coming to the
realization that "I am" unlike
no other

We are all children of God
fore the Lord Jesus Christ
he's not heavy, fore he is
my brother

Just Like Flowers

Have you ever touched
a rainbow
Have you ever kissed
the sky
Have you ever prayed
to Jesus, and then
began to
cry
Just like nature's
wondrous, majestic
beauty
For flowers care not
why

Simplicity

Money is to spend, and
gold is for the
rule
But a person without
love is just a simple
fool

Edward Scott

Deception Of Face

Spiritually polluted, genetically
diluted, historically degraded,
socially paraded
To digress from what we've
learned to transgress, and stir
up the feces of a species
Always a struggle to seek
eternal truth in life, I want a
divorce from social
strife
Such a diabolical brutal race
we've entered through
societies cycle of a vicious
game
To discover God's simplistic
love wins, which puts it all to
shame
Such a miracle given in life
some die, and never receive
from living a lie in brutality it's
love they really
need
It's a hostile race entered,
through the basic conception of being
good or bad
To worship the division of being
colored black or white, only to
find it's love we should have
had

When Worlds Collide

It's your world
squirrel, and I need more
than just
nuts
I've got my world, and
through lifes wicked trials,
and tribulations you've
got to have
guts
ally, ally, all come free
from sea to shiny sea, and
no you can't ride on
me
but I'll love you any way
this I will not hide, as long
as you respect my space
our worlds will not
collide

A Diluted Tale

Looking back on the annuls
of his story, one loses focus
on the real
glory
Swallowed up by the wooden
whale, with a poisoned mind,
a diluted
tale
Living day to day full of grief,
struggling to no
avail
Hard to forgive a soul, that seeks
adulterated, mind bending seasons
of unseasoned
relief
When sublived subliminal madness
is wild, and unforgiving of
such a nutured
belief

The Breeze And The Trees

As I listen to the soft serenade
of the song of the trees, during a
mellow evenings April
breeze
The sky is a bluish gray, and not
so lonely now, as the passing
clouds quicken my soul to
ease
The trees sing a song of serenity,
and peace, and the wind plays a
melodic calm, for all my troubles
to cease
Together they pose such a perfect
blend, to bless my soul, time and
time, begin

Ball Of Illusions

Women wanting to be men
men wanting to be women
billions squandered on
nothingness, and in the end
who's forgiven
The homeless is cents less,
but yet they still survive, so
when it comes to social hand
outs America takes
a dive
Priest raping young boys, and
lead the sheep they convert,
mere puppets, just like toys
getting off like
perverts
The rich getting away with
major crime, while the poor
do all the major
time
It's just a ball of illusions
hexed, It's what makes the
simple seem so
complexed
Then there's the victims of
this discrimination game, I call
it good versus evil, that's the
real name
Send men to the moon yet
people are starving, did Dahmer
pray before he started
carving
It's just a ball of illusions at its
best, divide and conquer, is the
game to suppress

So

If I am touched
do not I feel
cry havoc
For his story
be truly revealed,
and let time be
the medicine I
take
as I pray to God
for my soul to
truly wake
If I am of he, who
created me, my being
is truly blessed
So before I go, I'll
truly know
My being was not
as bad, as some
detest

Edward Scott

I Am

I am the hope and glory
soaring like a dove
I am the result of lost
dreams, antiquities spiritual love
I am the harvest of a crop
with a rich ancestral creed
I am the dream lost, with
true divine strength to succeed
I am the mystery of Egypt
land, who drank from the knowledge
of Pharaohs hand
I am the seed of antiquities
creed, from ancient astronauts,
pharmacologist, toxicologist, scientist,
scholars, engineers, agriculturist,
inventors of silent thoughts that touch
on command
I am conqueror of nations,
cities, communities, and states of mind,
body, and soul
I am to be labeled Black man
with historical riches yet to be told,
blessed beyond imagination, coming to
the realization that
I am

Displaced, Defaced And Erased

Time is the essence of man
one should savior

Change is the angel to embrace,
cold grows a soul who's unaware

When the lack of knowledge is
taken without care

Fore late recovery of a lost mind
in space, a life is always

Displaced, Defaced, and Erased

Fire Sale

I'll never love again, and
forever wonder why,
Theirs
a broken hearted
serenade I hear the lovers
cry
You can't hide, or buy love
when it's in the world, flying
like the wind, and on
fire
I'll never love again, and now
I'm cursed with this hard,
heavy, seething, mind throbbing
spirit called
desire

Thank God

This is not my world
but I am of the
world
I wish I was what I
used to be, fore now
I have to accept what
I am to
me
So even if you've lost,
and don't have a lot
Just thank God for what
you got

The Blessing

Some trust in golden chariots, and
worship green horses
I pray to trust in spiritual being, to
reap some real resources

As I went through the hell bank
I deposited some blood, sweat, and
tears

Then I layed me
down to sleep,
I wake to regrets
of unconscience
Fears

The interest was a soul retrieved like
an empty cup, fore like the deception
of a child, I grieved, and dranked the
knowledge up

I've loved dead hoes walking, fore
they carry a plenty of tale
Iniquitous lessons thought about that
may help me avoid a cell

God blesses his children of ill
repute, and touches one and all
Lift up who ever reads your work,
and let them stand, above it
all

The alpha bitch

We live in a world
between the beginnings, and
the ends

So where there's program
there's why's and so it all
begins

We open the doors to the
discovery of
lies

We've paid today, to pave
the way inwhich only the
strong survives

A Victims Run

To be young gifted, and hung,
bought like histories gold, my gift
of recognition is to get the story
told
To drink from the knowledge of
Kings, of yesterdays lessons
learned
To praise the sacrifices of sorrow
from those history have
burned
To be asleep we are like sheep, and
subject to a slaughter
Fore what shame we reap, the return
of Masa Bo Peep to enslave, our
fathers, mothers, sons,
and daughters
Knowledge is power, and education is
key, drink from the cup of the
knowledge of Kings, and set yourself
free
I did not, or do not choose to be your
victim, and that is your mistake, to
think me weak for all these years, just
for you to take
Just think when all is said and done
I'll pull your strings, a victims
run

Crashed And Turned

As we
slipped into the darkness, a
venture of a futureless jungle
plight, Through the windows of our
minds we view the twinkling of
sorrow, yonder due the light.
Fore at the blink of an eye the
treachery strikes like lightning,
an empty arena to no spiritual
rainbows
As trying we miss to kiss the sky,
flying high, to crash beyond low, and
still trying to reason why.
And all that's left for me tonight
is the fact that I crashed, and burned.
Misery loves company in a futureless
plight, and all users get is turned.

The Last Poem

From the prelude of a kiss, to
the ultimate pleasure of that
last exotic, tingling, tantalizing,
mind numbing, hypnotic
drooling, hump in the back
Oh God, oh God
bliss
This is the last poem, from the
beginning to the end
I am,
therefore I do transcend living,
loving, and learning how,
For the need more of love in life
is all I'm yearning now
So through the seasoning of the
years, I discover my souls true
tear's, fore letting go I triumph
over all my hidden
fear's.
This is the last poem,
until one day a child will say, as
he's a weeping real low.
He'll say "mom, and dad I feel
real glad, fore we break the
programmed mind to turn a souls
channeled view".
You've raised me good up under the
Son, now I pray to know
love true."

This is the last poem
until next time you see that boy
has turned into man, broad
shoulders, strong mind, and books
in hand.
So what's that I see in between
his story and chemistry, yes a
book on poetry.
So what you think new has already
been done, and as I transgress
through progress like hair through
a comb.
This is the last poem,
like a beautiful lady of love lost
This is the last poem,
like finally kissing her lips at
all cost.
This is the last poem,
like needing to touch this woman,
and so much more.
This is the last poem,
so to quote a poet of long before
I end this poem with
nevermore.

Generation Next

Years ago,
and some generations old
we lived, loved, and learned
through some worlds untold
So now,
the journey begins a new, to
try and save what lover's
are due
To discover,
a divine spiritual being
that's real, and all so
true
God's gift to us is, oh so
simple, but we make it, oh
so complex
It killed his only begotten
son, so the question is who's
next

M.E. *(Mysterious Element)*

Gently we go, just to
start again being foolish
in love, who? what? and
where is my friend's

Since the beginning of time
complexed comprehension of
simple compromised God like
apprehensions

As far as the milky way, and
as powerful, and majestic, like
a thunder bolt serenading to
caress a rainbows ray

The perfect man in a
imperfected sphere, there's a
myth called love, do you see
do you hear

Things change, but program
basically remains, fleeting
fad to material bad, just
because you think it's hip

Then theirs, that ever present
level of intellectual divide,
and conquer, to the jaded
program trip

It is I evolving into M.E.
with emotions locked away from
feelings of uneasy descent

Edward Scott

Weary, and astounded as I travel
the road of discovery, In search
of the metamorphi of the phenomeni
the Mysterious Element

True Form

Love is a form you can't
own, you can't cheat it, you
can't beat it
But just like life, love is
the partner you can't leave
alone
So to the unappreciative who
think they have it to use, abuse
or own
For the average mind you will
find, it's more than just meat
on a bone
The form will make you, or
break you, and leave you all
alone
Fly with your ego, and tear your
soul apart, crying, trying, dying
slowly, wishing for your
heart

Sirens Are Warnings

Once I saw a siren talking on
the pay phone, long black locks
hanging, deep dark, and beautiful
lovely, luscious tone

And as the epiphany glazed
at me, a look that would leave
madness misbehaving
It was in spite that I eased her
sight with a smile that would arrest
many a maiden

So I took the dare, and approached
the lonely vicious stare, with some
class-A stealth, and style
for the sun was bright, and my
mood, and M.O. was right, and I
knew I'd be awhile

And as our eyes met I began to
sweat, perspiring through my
sweater, so to break the
embarrassment of a monotonous
moment, I suggested a smile would
make it better

And so she acquiesced my gesture,
with such grace, and glare
Her beauty so astounded me, lost
in time, I did not care, to ease the
desires of my soul I took the vixens
dare

So as the voice of sultry, poetic
passions possessed my mortal soul,
It was my life I ended up giving, all
of my heart, body, mind, and gold

Edward Scott

Oh Freedom, My Freedom

Oh freedom, my freedom
how can I ever be the same
To have been where I've
been
To have heard what I've
heard
To have seen what I've
seen
To have lived love, and still
yearn
To recognize in my life, I'm
defined endangered species
a target for the
burn
Never again will I be sane, you
see where I've been was full
of deceit, a deep execution of
dark misery going beyond the
depth of a souls blame, shame,
and pain
If a witness had been, and heard,
and seen, and lived what I, surely
to escape, his reply
I die, I die, die I
til led to contemplate a conscience
lock down second by minute, by
hour, by day, by month, by year
in his head
Oh freedom, my freedom
without it I do not exist, for in
reality I'm dead

A Void That Stings

Living, a kiss
where the talk of passion
is a winter sting

Loving, a void that does not
exist, enter the imperial alter
called spring

Learning, a appetite for a true
spiritual call, fore without it we
are the nothingness of winter,
and spring is just like fall

U.F.O.s
Unidentified Frying Objects

Vapors, dreams, freaky triple
beams, many regrets from all,
as highs become syhs, bad good
buys, just before you fall
Clean up the temple fore now
it's cleansing time, slowing down
is to stand still, for the ringing of
the ethereal chime
So mind is right strong insight, to
avoid people, places, and things
like those, mental vapors untold
capers, attack of the

Bing, Bing, Bing U.F.O.s

Exstinct errors of political figures
feel the empty pockets void, as we
waste upon times of nothingness
just to become paranoid
Unidentified Frying Objects
is humanities shame, God made
not, man made so, for the green
eyed monsters game
So as the purple cow jumps over
the chocolate moon, glorifying the
lame, cripple, and crazy
I call to God to build me up
praying for the minds on this
planet to wake up, from being
bent, warped, and lazy

The Legend Of Spoatcoat

I'll tell you a story of a
mythical tale, that echoes
the incarcerated minds of
asylums, and jails

It deals with the silence of
the adulterated heart
locked away stories of vices,
which destroys the soul to
appreciate what's smart

From the annuls of antiquity
to the medieval chastity belt,
A man begins to take for
granted, a love that unbridled
raptures can melt

There never in this lifetime
will ever be, a natural born
player who is as good as he,

Fresher than cornflakes in milk
in a kinda hot, hot, sultry way,
you see he seduces diamonds for
the kiss of a cultured pearl, the
mark of this collectors day

So in an imperfect world, he cares
not how you be defined, go to jail,
get lost, dope out, or sexually
confused, and what's yours will truly
be the loss of mind

Echoes of untold silence, with quiet
storms blowing to ease her hidden
rapture, it's mans heart, and soul
that will pay, for his lack of love
has just been captured

Fore the tale is so fine about a
true player from the heart, I
thought you knew that you can't
trick a square, so you better
beware from the start

To be a pimp you're just a wimp
living off the weakness of women,
but a pimp is his biggest hoe, and
the game knows his booty is not
forgiven

So all you haters, and mental
rough necks beware, cause this
undisputed heavyweight player
is cashing checks, and the flesh,
and soul she'll bare

You better treat her right, because
he's like no other, you better hide
girlfriend, wife, sister, and your
mother

Man! she's the reason why, for love
we do, or die, in life the essence
is true, you take care of that which
takes care of you, or spoatcoat will
do his do

Merryhand Vanity Demands

Born to the rhythm of a passions
bloom, fore love, love, love I will
be consumed
I loved you in a place and time
a long, long dream ago
vanity became the vision, I soon
would come to know
And where it all began, I know
God didn't intend for love, true
love to inevitably end
Whatever happen to love, and
truly real concern, it got lost in
the shuffle of materialistic
superficial programs of yearn
I'll never love again, and heres
the reason why, you can't own
something that owns you, could
be why lovers cry
So while I'll never love again, though
it may be better to have not
heres to you the ones I tried, the
ones that time forgot
When I'm buried when my life is
through, I will forever regret, the
real love that I had for you, the
one time never forgets
So for now I'll never love again
at all cost, for an ethereal dream
named vanity, I wake to
abandonment, and no love
lost

Edward Scott

Fantasy People Get Real

Fantasy people make believe they
struggle with the prize, subjugation
individual nations, God sick them
open up their eyes

Integrity shocks, mental blocks just
because they commit to fools, the
ones that pay show real everyday,
and still get used like a tool

Raised of sufferage handed down
from shipped, whipped, slipped
morals of weird old schools

Fantasy people blaming mama,
and daddy for the hard love shown
Life was so fast it made them slow
for the spiritual, love that they have
blown

In Time

Rhythm and rhyme
from time to time
makes no difference
in the end
Failing minds, the ties
that bind, and in death
there's life
For love is where it
all begins

From Fried Skull
To Twinkle Toes

Passing up rim shots
for some fried skull
world cold, so grows
soul

I like my fried skull
served up bold

Kiss, kiss, Miss, miss
to the song of a twist

I'm getting, I'm getting
Iaaayy, Iaaayy got
steamy, hot glistening
rolls

Down to the balmy, moist
character of windows mist,
and twinkle toes

The Reign, The Pain, The Gain

What is life without
a little reign?

What is love when there
is no strain

Love me or leave me
hurt me or please me

The choices are yours
to
attain, when living, loving,
and learning how, one
must expect some
reign

Edward Scott

KTS Yesterday
KTS Tomorrow
KTS Forever

Yesterday,
My brother died, and by his side,
my mother cried, screaming silently, a look as if
something was ripping, tearing, stabbing,
aching transitions of pain on her face.

With nothing left to do, but try
an make his journey comfortably peaceful, and
serene as, he left this place

My brother died yesterday, and helpless,
powerless feelings of numbness, attacked every
being present.

The baby of my family, with no history of
ill, job related accident, who or what! Do we
resent or kill?

And as he got closer to leaving I heard him
say "why me" "lord why me!"

My love was lost, and I could not help but
to think, this should not be

And at that instant, I prayed to God.

To give him back his life, and let me take
deaths nod.

But at last, sparing with death was too
much for the spirit to take.

We prayed that he would be with God next
time when his soul would wake

My brother died yesterday, sad but true, my
father syhed, to a misery ride for the vultures
stride, tis all that lovers are due.

The Pecker Of the Monster From The Beast, Is Bleeding On The Wood

Life is a bitch, and she's
bleeding slowly through the
wood
Growing up playing cops,
and robbers, because somebody
said we should
Raised up on a small farm in
west Oakland, unlike others where
they raised, chicken, pigs, and
cattle
On this farm they raised people,
for bales, jails, and institutions, with
the struggle an immutable
battle
Minority of people basically good,
and the so called moral majority, the
green eyed monsters wishing that they
could
So it's not monkey see, monkey do
it's God loves me, and God loves
you
From the feces of a species, to a
toast to the beast, we have not only
been forcefully invited, but we are the
feast

Journey To Santa Rita

The journey to Santa Rita is like
a trip into the unknown, sometimes
I feel, I would like to go
home
But it is not long for tomorrow, and
tomorrow the day will come, I
know it is not long, but oh Lord
please let me go back
home
So this time I will walk carefully,
and watch my every step, oh Lord
be ready to help me if I should
slip
I lay on my bed remembering little
things, that don't seem worth much
thought,
but to me these kind of
memories are worth a lot, from
what the essence of time has
bought
So I'll keep them to recall the simple
things when I feel a little low
Oh Lord, Oh Lord,
let me go, let me go

By Joyce Ervin

TOMORROW, TOMORROW
By Joyce Ervin

I love you in all my ways, but
sometimes I don't know where
I stand
I hate saying goodbye
that makes me cry, for the
happenings in the past, but life
goes on by
Those days are past, and what
we had better do is
live, and make the most out of
the life we have to
give

Edward Scott

Niggers

It's not so much as
that racist white man
that I'm worried
about
It's just his enigmas
that scare me to
death

"Thou Shall Not Think"
By James Scott

From the doctrines of everyday life
dictates to you, me, and even my
wife
No room to wonder, ponder, or even
wink, in a state where thou shall not
think
Invisible crimes committed in every
way, no time to think, nothing to say,
Why? oh why? is life that of
clay
Provisionally concentrating on what,
and why you, and I duel
Keeping our thoughts in our own
social whirlpool
So tell me how, one can raise up out
of the slime in the sink?
In a state where thou shall not
think
The wars we fight are no concern of
ours considering cocaine has hit us
hard, not looked upon as equals to
peers, for fear of injustice over the
years
Yet you holler this land is for me, when
sister's, and brothers die in the streets
immutably
This is the land you stake your pride
not noticing the individuals snickering
on the side
Of course you are the product of their
deceit, living in a state where thou
shall not think

This Heart
By James Scott

This heart can only be satisfied
by the juices that you flow
embracing you like never, never,
ever before
L-0-V-E
that is my cure, to a woman naturally
mines, and this I feel and know
for sure even at uncertain
times
Devoted soulfully, yes!
I am to a divine woman, gentle as a
lamb, as I cry silently while sitting
in the slam
Talking with your picture softly,
spiritually walking with thee, while
some people perambulate in their
minds thinking I'm crazy
Charged by forces of this ol heart, I
pray that we may never, never, ever
part, fore if such a departure
transpires, may I burn in the hottest
of hells, and deepest of
fires
Fore the "Most High" has blessed
me, with an eternal craving, and a
glow so true, truthfully I Love
You
So now, this heart is for you, to do
as you please, may my tear's stream
from joy, and heart at
ease
This is how much you mean to me
This Heart

AT ONE POINT
By James Scott

History did not mean a thing
to me, now I realize what others
never dreamed, they labeled
"US"
As savages, Negroes, Afrikan
American Blacks, degrading to
our progress, and these are the
facts
Stripped of our culture, religion,
and love, to a home not controlled
by "US"
The first to achieve the degree
of thought, building, civilization for
people to survive, befriended a
nation that told "US"
lies
It's sad for me to understand, how
could man enslave another man?
Our women experienced something
worse than the Afrikan fate, forced
to have sex with a lighter
mate
The children separated with tears
in their eyes, destined for things that
never happened to you or the other
guys
So here in the nineties, life is about
the same, it is us killing each other
without no shame
No need for shacklets, whips, or
chains, do to the average persons
lack of brains

Edward Scott

No principals, morals, or even
respects so how do you rise above all
the rejects, all the mess?, when all you
think about is getting undressed
My love, or friends are all black
Americans, in the home of the
Braves,
It was my ancestors not me who were Afrikan
American slaves
separated from a nation that was vast
it's time to remember our glorious
past

Passions Secrets Unleashed

I don't know why, I feel like
I do, could it be the due, that
you do, that I'm due when with
you
Secrets of passions unleashed
by your infinite beauty, that
knows the heart beyond leaps,
and bounds, to the depths of
a souls ethereal love
The smile of love upon my
heart, sings with silent raptures
for the waiting of your return
The feelings of empty existence
wreak havoc upon my being, fore
now it's you I yearn
I don't know why I feel you like
I do, fore your essence breaks
down barriers, built by timeless
deities freaky unbalance, just to
have a clue
Around here in my heart, without
your space, and time
The things you present to a mans
heart should most definitely be a
crime
Where is she to be "ol Lord"
Where is she for me "ol Lord"
What am I?
mind, soul, and nobody
so why did you use my body, for
your own physical realm
of lust, and leave my heart empty,
soul unfulfilled, and mind cloudy

like a constipated stigma full of
waste like rust
Didn't I love you good, from my
head, to the twinkling of your toes
So why the mistreatment of heartless
things you know! players like those
So as I die from lovely, luscious hugs,
with kisses of doom, your love is
killing me softly, so my heart is now
consumed
Before I die a question of why
Is it all fair in love and war
Why me, did I lie, and why does my
heart require you
more
Echoes of silence as the windows of
my soul's view deteriorates to your
absence, fore now time stands still
fore it's the energy that you present
that moves me like
the world
To create a man to nothingness, for
nuts are just the food of Gods, and
the conquest is just for
squirrels

The Quickening

I personify I
The realization of a functioning
spirit

Living, Loving and learning
is what I wish to achieve.
While understanding my human nature
without material greed.

To wake is like a quickening of the
mind, body and soul.
To find my true identity before
I grow old.

Conscious confrontation with
my sub-conscious.
Now I know, with each new day I
want to grow

Negativity no longer exist.
Only the true positive awareness
of one love I persist

Mentally hungry no more chain's
my bodies the temple in which
I will not strain.

A good brain washing is easy
to find.
I just want to use my own
mind.

Sublimenal holocaust which started
from birth, just because my
parent's were first

Positive thoughts come a while
so I may discover the golden child

Just a Moment

Just as happy as I
can be.
A feeling of such
content

It's like a natural
high of such great
extent

Shall I not enjoy this
moment
before it ends,
before the opposite
begins

Edward Scott

Unthinkably You

To touch you with my eye's
is pleasure beyond
control

To hold such beauty in my
mind, I'm tempted to get
bold

A curse, my body registers
like a rising sun,
the heat of passion has
just begone

I began to sweat, knowing
that to love you is
forbidden.

While I attempt to mask
these feeling's I have
hidden

Lust in my heart, breaks
with disgust

Oh yes!
I must, I must.

Kiss you lip's like the
whispering wind.

Hold you close let me in
let me come inside your
soul.

Till mind and body are one
reaction and the feeling
grows cold

You are forbidden fruit
a thought that can't be
nursed.

So I accept the fact that
I am cursed

Tales, Tail's, Tell

New faces, new places,
discoveries of lost world's
and wiped out
races

One must obtain culture
in order to achieve
Only then will one rise,
above those who
deceive

So study different world's
of an experienced
fact

Fore what Tale's Tail's Tell,
find fiction to be exact

Drop The R

My friend's dropped the R,
they drop the R.

My friend's dropped the R,
can't you read?

A social injustice immoral
respect,
they dropped the R

No responsibility, spiritual reject,
they dropped the R

Lack of education Perennial
neglect,
they dropped the R

An unorthodoxed parallel,
eventually they'll go to
hell, can you
read?

My friend dropped the R
if you know what I
mean
and that spells
F-I-E-N-D
R

Edward Scott

From Natural's to Unnaturals

What do you call an
African American, who
turns on his sister, and
brother man?

An abomination!

The personification of
the worst enemy of
the black race, is that
neo-nazi with the
black face

A freak against nature,
loving strife
living an unholy
sacrificial life

It brings to one's mind
the Anti-christ

Soul Creator

As roses are beautiful,
so must you
be
Lovely, Luscious Lady

A delectable Queen,
creator of my universe.
One of nature's sweetest
nectar's I must
nurse

Beautiful lady
surely you must know that
without you my soul would
not grow

With your
Lovely, luscious little
whirl, it's how you started
in this girl.

So look NOW?
Beautiful, Lovely, Luscious,
mother of pearl.

Sweeter than the sweetest
strawberries
and more desirable than a
basket full of
cherries

Edward Scott

To define the word "LOVE"
I think of you, and wonder if
Mr. Webster had you in mind
Too

A Game for All Reasons

As a child,
you learn to play
games

It is the epitome of
reasoning
you play to get
seasoning.

As you grow, the games
become serious

You must be quick to
understand, or your play
could seem
delirious

It is something that starts
at birth, and keeps
on going.

Until you leave this
EARTH

Wear Quality Genes

What's in those genes?
It makes me wonder
From Afrikan grandeur to
American trickonmics, and
behavior

What's in those genes?
could be a perverted thought
Makes me wonder about when
I came out

If my inheritance must come
from the genes.
Lets hope the materials was
of high quality spiritual
human beings

What's in those genes?
Could be pads for confidence,
of phony fad of something
never had

It's so Ironic, yet so true,
This could explain the acts
that some do

As I grow older, I will continue
to ponder
What's in those genes?
A mysterious wonder

As I watch certain family, and
friend's in their genes
I envy not their personal
being

Freestyle. Funnystyle. Buckwild
who knew?

Are you wearing your genes or
are your genes wearing
you.

Apology "Keep Dreaming"

I'll accept an apology
how about you?
An apology, and more, is
long over
due

If I raped your grand
mother's mother down to
your wife's sister's
daughter

Castrated is what I'd
be and still would you
not deserve an
apology

Four hundred and some
odd years of
rape
By the blue eyed hairless
ape

Sabotage my cultural
right,
bought and sold I've
inherited the fight

Before I die of blind
stupidity
I demand retribution, in
the form of an apology,
money and land.
40 acres and a mule
at hand

Pure Love and Money

I thought I was freed
from slavery a long
time ago.

But then you want to
tax me, like I'm some
ass hole

So forget the what, and
why
Just give me some
P U. S. S. I.

Love and money
goes hand in hand
But people who got
it just don't
understand

To be meek, doesn't
mean that your weak.
It's a concern, that
you learn
when you get your turn,
to earn
some P U. S. S. I.

Yeah! and then they say,
the "MEEK SHALL INHERIT
THE EARTH"

I think the freaks will
do it first

A Blessing

Angel of deliverance show me
the way to peace, happiness
and a beautiful
day

Help me in my discovery, and
keep me strong during
recovery

Fore life has no meaning
without spiritual truth,
understanding and wisdom, it's
a blessing that's the
proof.

So let me wake before I die.
Guide me away from the miseries,
the shortcomings and the
mighty lie

Grant me the awareness of my
spiritual best, keep my mind,
body and soul positive, away
from the evil
rest

Angel of deliverance
I thank you, and with
GOD's strength I now know
what to do.

IN MEMORY of DEACON PERCY BESS

The Good, The Bad, The America

America cheats her old,
look out folk's or you
could be in the
cold

America beats her young,
look out whore,
they have
gun's

America supports drugs
How else do you explain
billion dollar political
thugs

America taxes labor to
death makes the average
worker gasp for
breath

America doesn't take
care of it's own, but if
your'er a foreigner,
you can sit on a golden
throne

You might think that I'm
kind of bitter,
what the hell I'm an American
and it's hard to
quit her

Edward Scott

Shadow Cross

I can't find my shadow,
and I'm scared to death.

Am I dead?
Have I taken my last
breath?

Must find my shadow, my
familiar at best, or be
condemned to gloom, with
no eternal rest

It was always there when
in doubt, in need, or in
total despair

I've lost my shadow, how
could this be?
To lose something that's part
of me

It was always there,
during the darkest of days,
even at night, in the light,
of my addicted
way's

You know something is wrong,
when your shadow is
gone

Did it leave because of a
mission of habit,

or am I experiencing my
shadow's Sabbath

If you should see my shadow
before I do, tell it I'm
sorry and miss one so
spiritually true

I must see my shadow and real
soon before I kill myself
trying to reach the
moon

Paying Dues Within

As I peer out the window
of an incarcerated room
I think of a world
full of gloom

I see a road abandoned, with
looks of doom

From the inside I peer such
noise I hear as the victimless
men come out their
gates

They snarl and stare at the
food prepared and then they
perambulate.

Led by this double edge sword
called society some live for
the immoral indifferent,
perversion of jail notoriety

As I pay my due's within. I
make no excuses.
It was my fault for my misuse
and abuses.

So I pay my due's and seek
not to use, iniquitous vehicles
of self destruction

And with a syh of relief I'll
have no grief, when I leave
These victimless men
of corruption

Feeling's of Want

I want to hold your tenderness
in my arm's
Caress your voluptuous awareness
with my charms

Kiss your lovely, luscious lip's
to mine, as if to taste a sweet
virgin wine

I want to make wild, passionate,
love to your mental,
with the intent to improve, on the
rapture of ecstasy's physical
potential

I want echoes of love when I
think of you
Beautiful, voluptuous, tender twin
peaks too

Not to mention, those firm cheek's
and hip's
So to speak, of those luscious
lip's echoes love, love, love lust
from the start.

I love you it's firmly in my
heart
Echoes of love, I thank GOD for
you Such a fabulous lady, a wonder
that's true.

Paradise Had You

LIFE! A reflection of a dream
I once knew
From the womb of paradise I
live, should not they be worthy,
I forgive.

As a child the stage is set, to
live love and learn Fore the
little things I missed to regret
it's the simple things
I yearn.

LIFE! A reflection of iniquitous
lesson, of where there's good.
so will the bad be real, yet so
far from giving
A lesson often thought about,
when life is of
sub-living

LIFE! The temptations of a bad dream
I knew To the spoon. I learned to
use
While devouring life's immutable
temptous nature, I now stand
abused

An act right out of painful
memories at times when censured
and used

So the spoon I stooped and thrived,
serving a craving of an unnatural
instinct, in order to
survive

LIFE! The repentance of a dream
I knew, of a tripartite soul, with
miles of tear's.
The need more of more life.
with little ignorance. poverty
and fear's

So it's the tomb I go, with no
disguise eternally wishing I
never left paradise

Cracker Of The Nineties

Head crack and glass,
is what you are

At once upon a time,
you were a star

Your life was so
postive, full of hope.

Head crack and ass,
now you're a joke

Your life was so
wonderful, full and
together

Now you walk the streets.
in any kind of'
weather

The living dead, you
know it's true

Head crack and glass.
your life is
through

Lord Help Me

Oh Lord
Help me to see, that
which my eye's cannot
see

Help me lord, help me to hear
that which my ear's
cannot hear

Oh merciful GOD, fill my
heart with your love, and let
it overflow, and touch that
which cannot be
touched

Oh Lord, Oh Jesus help me
because I love like you so
much

O.D. On The T.V.

O.D. on the T.V. now there's a
place I don't want to be, looking
at all that hyped up
misery.

O.D. of T.V
Am I looking at your program or
are you watching actual
program of
me.

O.D. on the T.V.
Like junkies we smile and stare at
misery most prepared, for the
visual entertainment of man made
ghouls, watch out and
beware

O.D. of T.V.
ECHOES murder, death, kill
echoes murder, death, kill

No peace, no love plenty of violence,
hate and gore,
Oooh turn the channel lets
find some more,
like an oozing sore
it s more than just a rating
war.

O.D. on the T.V.
I can no longer bare bizarre,
cruel, and unusual

Keeps a viewer so miserably
unaware, of the love and happiness
out there

Street Love

I was married to the
streets once upon a
time

Full of grief,
Full of crying.

She can be deceitful
jealous, bitter, and
cold.
Then she'll reveal her
rage and steal your
soul

I was blind and innocent
hers at will,
It was the slick ones she
made pay for the priviledge
when she made her
kill.

So a warning I give you
before you say
adieu

the streets she's full of
fire, she'll turn you out
with the wink of
desire,
and before you get
a chance for your
drools and sighs

She will bury you cold with
the shake of her
hips and highs

Crack House Blues

I've seen Elvis at the
rock house acting kind
of strange

So I pulled him to the
side and said, man you
are way out of
range

He looked me up and down
and then on his knees
to the floor, where he
scrounged around

He looked up at me and
gave me some rythme,
and started singing
the blues.

Boy let me warn you
about spreading this news
No one will believe you
and don't go steppin
on my new suede
shoe's

I've seen Elvis and he
had the crack house
blues

A Spiritless Friend

Loneliness is a friend of
mine, from place to place
and time to time

In a room full of people
there I'll find, loneliness
that friend of mine.

Sometimes I avoid it with
censure, but somehow it finds
me and takes me on an
adventure

Loneliness is a friend of
mine, even in love it sneaks
up at the wrong time

I even threw parties to put
it to a test, and found
loneliness the only real
guest.

The one true thing in life
I find, is that everyone needs
some-body from time to time.

And while everything has it's
own rhythm and rhyme, I find
loneliness a real friend of
mine.

Strip Critics

Critics of strife
full of advice

Always want to tell
you about your
life

What little concern
do they show, about
the want's the need's
which only the individual
knows

Fore what you think, is
not for me to give.

It's for me to have faith
and be the best that I
can be, and
live

The Embrace of Stormy Wheather

The lesson learned of yesterdays
stormy whether, brings the reasons
yearned for the satisfaction of
why.

Embraced should be todays sunnyside,
fearing not the lessons learned,
fore satisfactions can make
a soul cry

But the reasons yearned for walking
in a righteous plight, bare possibilities
of a true spiritual awakening, out
of the dark, and into the
light.

This you do over and over again
or die goes the soul within
Which makes it hard to
live again

Edward Scott

Bother's or Brother's

My brother's song I hear
through my heart
Living, Loving, and Learning
everyday, and blessed with a
brand new start.

From scared times that were
scuffled upon my face,
to the scares you scuffled upon
my heart

Let time be the medicine I
take to heal, and to the
heart that love has filled,
more remains to be
revealed.

As a sleeper awakens to change
so will the awareness be, my
brother's song I hear again
and pray for serenity.

I feel the power of love, which
will surely heal, for, you sing
a song of hurt and pain that can
love or eventually
kill.

The Nothingness of A Man

We waste upon times of nothingness…
unwilling to prepare, for the
sagacious blossoming of a spiritual
being,
so rich, but yet so
unaware.

The nothingness of a souls
inhumanity
From the idioms of antiquity, a will not
broke in stride,
It causes one to be lonely, with
rage bottled up
inside.

We waste upon a point in time, where
just a mere existence falls heavy
on one's mind.

As you look deep into the eye's of
nothingness, and wonder upon a gaze,
of why now and not then does
conscienceness so
amaze.

The nothingness of man's existence
only in materialistic superficial
gain.
Things of inanimate significance of
a greed some die
to attain.

The things we think are new
we do,
yet and still they've already been
done.

We waste upon times of nothingness, and
just think, GOD gave his only
begotten son

In Search Of The Invisible Men

I've seen the invisible men,
they'er living in warehoused
land.

Locked away from variety, by
a system that lacks truth,
An injustice of a spiritually
cultured society.

In this warehoused incarceration,
I see the invisible men
speak,
Their mouths are moving but
their words are weak

Ostracized'

Should not they be
meek?

They won't be heard, such a
wrong time to
speak.

An abomination who knew?
What such a creation,
would lead
too.

A majority of the minorities
lost generations.
I've seen the invisible men

Edward Scott

Who, What, Where, and Why?
Only if you dare to try,
Only if you care to try

About the Author

Edward Scott a poet/writer extraordinaire, is a product from the beautiful metropolis of Oakland, California. A graduate of McClymonds High School, Airco Technical Institute, and the prestigeous Merritt College. He attended Cole Elementary School, there the prodigy was first printed, at the ripe old age of 10 years young. His first poem was published by, the Oakland Post Newspaper,Circa 1970. It was entitled "My Dream for My Country", in which he not only won an award, but received a letter of recognition, from the Governor of Oregon for such a sensitive work of literary prose. He further extended his writing talents, by working for Youths In Action, a teen news letter about urban life in the glorious city of Oakland, CA. And now 33 years later, destiny has run it's course, in which Mr. Scott brings to you the reader, truth in the form of a spiritual awakening.

Where there's *NO REASONABLE EXPLANATION REQUIRED Vol.I* and *THE AFTERBIRTH Vol.II* and last but not least *THE METAMORPHI OF THE PHENOMENI Vol.III*

STAY TUNED